The Battle of Saratoga

by Don Nardo

Content Adviser: Robert Bruce, Ph.D.,
Department of History,
Sam Houston State University

Reading Adviser: Rosemary G. Palmer, Ph.D.,
Department of Literacy, College of Education,
Boise State University

Compass Point Books ✦ Minneapolis, Minnesota

Compass Point Books
3109 West 50th Street, #115
Minneapolis, MN 55410

Visit Compass Point Books on the Internet at *www.compasspointbooks.com*
or e-mail your request to *custserv@compasspointbooks.com*

On the cover: *The Battle of Saratoga* by Andy Thomas (detail)

Editor: Mari Bolte
Page Production: Ashlee Schultz
Photo Researcher: Svetlana Zhurkin
Cartographer: XNR Productions, Inc.
Library Consultant: Kathleen Baxter

Creative Director: Keith Griffin
Editorial Director: Nick Healy
Managing Editor: Catherine Neitge

Library of Congress Cataloging-in-Publication Data
Nardo, Don, 1947–
  The Battle of Saratoga / by Don Nardo.
     p. cm. — (We the people)
  Includes bibliographical references and index.
  ISBN-13: 978-0-7565-3342-7 (library binding)
  ISBN-10: 0-7565-3342-2 (library binding)
1. Saratoga Campaign, N.Y., 1777—Juvenile literature. I. Title.
  E241.S2N37 2008
  973.3'33—dc22   2007004597

TABLE OF CONTENTS

Preparing to Stop the Enemy

In August and early September 1777, British General John Burgoyne led a powerful force of 7,800 troops through upstate New York.

About 3,300 of these troopers were well-equipped British fighters called Redcoats because of their bright red uniforms. Around 3,900 of Burgoyne's men were mercenaries from Germany. British leaders wanted them to help control Britain's 13 American colonies. The other 600 troops were Canadians fighting for the British.

Burgoyne's mission during this war between Great Britain and its colonies was to travel south through the Hudson River Valley

British General John Burgoyne

4

and capture American forts and towns.

But the colonists, who knew the British were heading their way, had set up a strong defensive barrier and were massing their own troops around it. Each day more colonial soldiers arrived. They came not only from New York, but also from New Hampshire, Vermont, Massachusetts, Connecticut, and as far away as Virginia. Some American troops chopped down trees to block the dirt roads on which Burgoyne's men marched. This slowed the British advance by as much as a mile per day.

The American troops were near the town of Saratoga, which was 35 miles (56 kilometers) north of Albany, New York.

American General Horatio Gates

General Horatio Gates, commander of the American forces, ordered his chief engineer, Thadeusz Kosciuszko, to make sure that Bemis Heights received proper fortifications.

Close to the Hudson River, Bemis Heights was the highest hill in the vicinity. From its flat, wooded summit, one could see for many miles in all directions. Although the hill had been named after the owner of a local tavern, the property belonged to a farmer named John Neilson, who had a small house and log barn atop the hill. Neilson was now a soldier under Gates' command. Gates chose the barn to be his base camp and fortified it by stationing troops around it. Out of respect for the farmer who wanted to defend his home, Gates named the barn Fort Neilson.

Gates had chosen this place for good reason. He knew that the only road leading southward toward Albany passed between the hill and the river. This meant that Burgoyne must pass by Bemis Heights. By September 15, 1777, the Americans were prepared to stop the enemy. Kosciuszko and his men had erected an earthen barrier at the top of the hill. Gates had placed a battery of cannons at each end. The Americans also dug a trench across the road near the tavern and placed cannons behind the trench.

The British approached these stout defenses in the cold, damp morning of September 19. At that moment,

Neilson Farm at Saratoga National Historical Park

Burgoyne's army camped near Saratoga.

neither they nor the American soldiers could foresee the
ultimate importance of the bloody battle they were about to
fight. Historians would view it as the great turning point of
the Revolutionary War.

BRITAIN'S ATTACK PLAN

As Burgoyne's army approached Saratoga in September 1777, the colonists had been fighting the British for more than two years. The first battles of the American Revolutionary War occurred in April 1775. What led to the fighting were several disputes that had erupted between Britain and its 13 American colonies.

Among other disagreements, many colonists felt that the British had taxed them unfairly. Protests, some of them violent, occurred

Colonists protested at an anti-Stamp Act demonstration in 1765.

9

in several of the colonies in the late 1760s and early 1770s. In 1774, the British wanted to punish the colonists and shut down the most prosperous port in the colonies—the Port of Boston. They also forced Americans to lodge British soldiers in their homes.

These actions only angered the colonists more. On May 17, 1774, some colonial leaders, including George Washington and Thomas Jefferson, met to discuss how to react. They boldly declared: "An attack made on one of our sister colonies is an attack made on all British America."

Tensions continued to mount until April 19, 1775, when an outbreak of bloody skirmishes between British troops and armed colonists took place at Lexington and Concord in Massachusetts. These battles marked the point of no return for the colonies. On July 4 of the following year, they declared themselves free of British control through the Declaration of Independence.

Britain was not ready to give up its colonies without a fight. Troops were sent to strengthen its existing army in

General George Washington led the Continental Army during the Revolutionary War.

America. The colonists did not do well in the early battles. The Americans were outgunned, and many of them lacked military training and experience. American General George Washington did manage to score some minor victories

Washington's Continental Army won its first victory at the Battle of Trenton on December 26, 1776.

during the winter of 1776–1777.

However, many leaders in America and across Europe still believed that the colonists had little chance of winning the conflict.

With this in mind, British leaders hatched a plan designed to ensure an American defeat. General Burgoyne would march his army southward from Canada toward New

12

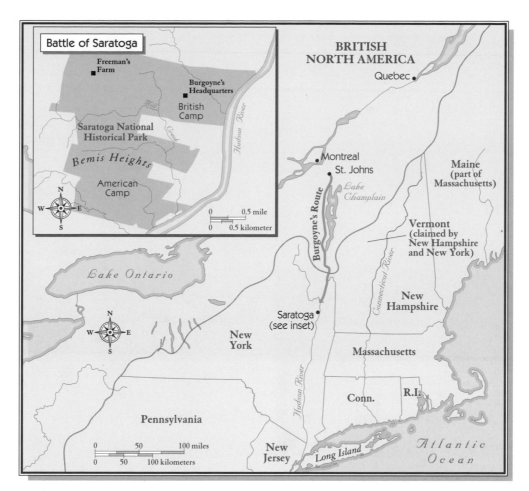

Burgoyne's army marched south from Canada through New York with the intent of dividing the Northeast from the rest of the colonies.

York City, capturing one town or fort after another. The goal was to cut off the colonies in the Northeast from the rest of the colonies. This would weaken the Americans by making it difficult for them to coordinate a united war effort.

13

Cannons are displayed at the Saratoga National Historical Park in New York.

Confident of victory, Burgoyne left Canada in July 1777 with a well-trained army and an impressive array of weapons. One of his officers described the artillery as "the finest and probably the most excellently supplied" cannon train he had ever seen.

What Burgoyne and his countrymen did not take into account was the determination and bravery of the enemy soldiers they would soon face.

READY TO FIGHT

When American leaders learned that General Burgoyne was moving southward from Canada, they were determined to stop him. Washington knew that this would require many troops. Some members of the Continental Army were already stationed in the upper Hudson River Valley. Continentals were full-time soldiers who received training and usually wore standard uniforms.

On August 19, 1777, General Horatio Gates took charge of these troops. To help him, Washington sent some soldiers led by Major General Benedict Arnold and another force commanded by Major General Benjamin Lincoln.

At the same time, Washington asked the colonies to send as many militiamen as they could spare. Militiamen, or militia, were part-time soldiers, most often farmers and merchants. When needed, they would grab their weapons, march off to fight, and then return to their homes and families when the emergency was over. Answering

15

Militiamen left their homes and families behind to fight the British.

Washington's call, militiamen from far and wide met in the area of Saratoga. Gates eventually commanded about 15,000 men. Of these, perhaps half were Continentals and half were militiamen.

Gates' forces eventually outnumbered Burgoyne's. However, as leaders on both sides realized, sheer numbers were not necessarily a decisive factor. Most of the British soldiers had more training than the Americans. Also, Burgoyne had more and better cannons than Gates did. These factors gave the British a real chance to achieve success in the campaign.

Militiamen were citizen soldiers.

But there was another factor that both surprised and disturbed Burgoyne and other British leaders. This was the overall effectiveness of the American militiamen. At the start of the conflict, the British had viewed these men as untrained and undisciplined. The British were used to fighting wars against enemies in Europe. There, when armies of trained soldiers marched through an area, the frightened farmers and other civilians usually hid or ran away.

17

Militamen, along with the regular Continental Army, came from all over the colonies to fight together.

In colonial America, by contrast, British troops were constantly annoyed and harassed by civilian fighters. Burgoyne complained, "Wherever the King's forces point, militia to the number of three or four thousand assemble in a few hours." Not only were the militiamen unafraid to fight, but they also sometimes used guerrilla tactics, which the British were not used to. British soldiers commonly fought in organized units on open battlefields. Most

Militiamen knew how to use their surroundings to their advantage with great success, often ambushing the British.

militiamen did so, too. But when the tactic was appropriate, many of these militiamen also fought as individuals and fired from behind trees and rocks.

Each American soldier, Burgoyne observed, is "his own general, who will turn every tree and bush into a kind of temporary fortress." With thousands of such soldiers gathering near Saratoga, Burgoyne had good reason to be worried.

MORGAN'S DEADLY RIFLEMEN

Besides the bravery of the American militiamen, General Gates had another advantage. He commanded one of the most effective units in the military. It was a group of 400 riflemen led by Colonel Daniel Morgan of Virginia.

A tall, burly man with a fiery temper, Morgan had earned a reputation fighting the British during the failed American invasion of Canada in 1775. He and his men played a pivotal role in the fight at Saratoga and would become legendary in the American Revolution.

Part of what made Morgan and his men unusual soldiers were the weapons they wielded—rifles. At the time, the rifle was an uncommon firearm that few people owned or knew how to use. Most troops still used muskets. A musket fired when a spark from a piece of flint ignited a tiny pan of gunpowder. Muskets were seen as fairly reliable in open battle, partly because they could be reloaded and fired two or three times a minute. In contrast, early rifles

Daniel Morgan was skilled in military tactics and planning.

took almost an entire minute to load.

But the rifle did have one important advantage over the musket. It was more accurate. The inside of a musket's

Morgan's troops were trained to be skilled marksmen.

barrel was smooth. The metal ball unleashed by the gunpowder wobbled as it moved through the barrel. As a result, the ball left the weapon off-center, making accurate shots difficult. In contrast, the inside of a rifle's barrel featured spiral grooves known as rifling, which gave the weapon its name. When fired, the ball fit tightly inside the grooves and left the rifle on-center. This made the weapon much more likely to hit its target.

Morgan's riflemen were trained as expert marksmen, and they could easily hit a 7-inch (17.8 centimeter) target at a distance of 250 yards (227.5 meters), which is the length of two and a half football fields. Morgan adopted the tactic of placing his men in or behind trees. They would pick off British soldiers, particularly the officers, at a great distance. The British soldiers felt the intentional targeting of officers was morally wrong, and the government in Britain labeled Morgan a war criminal.

Most soldiers used muskets.

George Washington saw Morgan as a treasured asset to his army, and he dispatched the group of riflemen to Saratoga. Writing to Gates on August 20, 1777, Washington said, "This corps I have great dependence on and have no doubt that they will be exceedingly useful." This proved to be an

23

American marksmen in trees fired at British soldiers.

understatement. At Saratoga, Burgoyne and his troops
would discover the terrible damage the American riflemen
could inflict.

STRUGGLE FOR FREEMAN'S FARM

On the morning of September 19, 1777, General Burgoyne's army was camped less than two miles (6.4 km) from Bemis Heights, where the American troops were stationed. But the two armies could not see one another. Thick woods, low hills, and ravines lay between them. A heavy fog had blanketed the area that morning, making it difficult to see or navigate more than a few yards in any direction.

Using the fog to his advantage, Burgoyne ordered an advance force to creep up on the American camp. He sent one of his most trusted officers, General Simon Fraser, with about 1,000 soldiers through the woods to the edge of Freeman's Farm. The small farmhouse and sheds sat in the middle of a large clearing, about a mile (1.6 km) north of Bemis Heights. When Fraser arrived at the clearing, it was early afternoon and the fog had lifted.

As more British troops approached his position from the north, Fraser decided to seize the farm. He sent a

British General Simon Fraser

battle-hardened officer, Major Gordon Forbes, with 100 men to scout the area. Forbes did not realize that he was walking into a trap. Less than an hour before, Daniel Morgan's riflemen had hidden themselves in and around the farm. As the British approached, American snipers opened fire. Several of Forbes' men fell dead, and Forbes himself was wounded.

As Forbes and his surviving men retreated, Morgan's fighters jumped from their hiding places and gave chase. When they reached the heavily armed British lines, Morgan issued a loud "gobble-gobble," his imitation of a turkey.

26

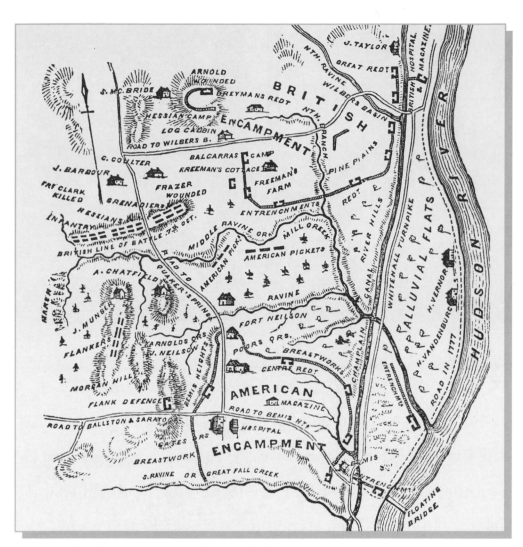

A map of the battleground near Freeman's Farm

This was the signal to fall back into the woods, which his men did. From their new hiding places, they were able to fire well-aimed shots, killing many British officers.

Morgan's men fought the British at the edge of Freeman's Farm.

At this point, Benedict Arnold sent two units of
American Continentals to aid Morgan. These soldiers pushed
the British to the edge of the woods and Freeman's Farm.
But they were unable to break through the British line and
had to fall back. Then Arnold himself led a furious charge.

One of the American soldiers later recalled seeing
Arnold "riding in front of the lines, his eyes flashing,
pointing with his sword ... with a voice that rang clear
as a trumpet and electrified the line." This inspired the

American troops to fight harder.

Despite Arnold's heroics, he too was unable to penetrate the British lines. Late in the afternoon, Burgoyne's German troops, led by General Frederick Riedesel, appeared. The arrival of these fresh soldiers discouraged any further American attacks. The first phase of the Battle of Saratoga was over. No one realized that the second phase would prove bloodier and more decisive.

American General Benedict Arnold

THE FIGHT AT BEMIS HEIGHTS

At the end of the day on September 19, 1777, the British controlled most of Freeman's Farm. But about 600 British soldiers had been killed in battle, compared with American losses of only 300. Burgoyne was unsure about the enemy's troop strength. He was beginning to suspect that he was seriously outnumbered, so he delayed his next attack. His strategy was to wait until another British general, Henry Clinton, arrived. Believing that Clinton was leading a small relief force northward along the Hudson River, Burgoyne sat waiting for three weeks. In reality, by this time Clinton had turned back.

As the days went by, Burgoyne's situation became increasingly desperate. His supplies grew thin, and his soldiers' morale fell. Meanwhile, the American army continued to grow. Burgoyne's officers urged him to retreat, but he refused. Perhaps hoping to save face, he unwisely ordered an all-out attack on Gates' camp at Bemis Heights.

Benedict Arnold (on horseback on the right) encourages his troops at the Battle of Saratoga.

Riedesel's Germans began the assault late on the morning of October 7. Not far behind them came Fraser's unit, followed by another battalion.

On the hill, the Americans were fully prepared to

31

meet the attack. General Lincoln's units suddenly poured a devastating round of musket fire into the enemy lines. As the Germans and British soldiers faltered, Lincoln's men charged forward. According to one observer, the Americans "poured down like a torrent from the hill." They were able to push the attackers back, capturing several of their cannons.

American General Benjamin Lincoln

Meanwhile, to the west of this struggle, Morgan's deadly riflemen assaulted Fraser's troops. One of the

American sharpshooters took aim at Fraser and shot him. The badly wounded British officer was carried from the field and died later that day.

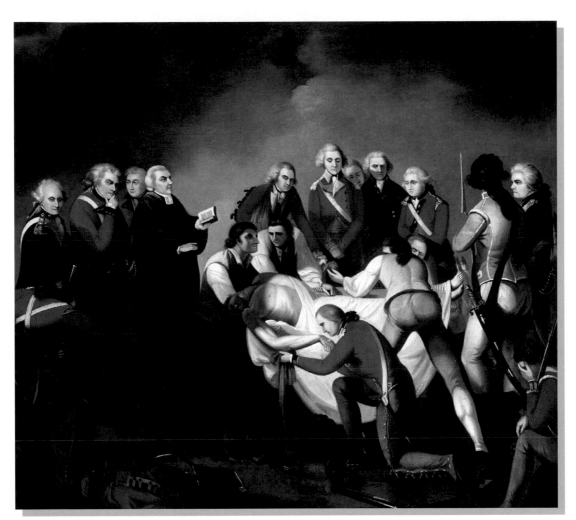

General Simon Fraser was buried on the battlefield after the Battle of Saratoga.

33

*Benedict Arnold defended himself after being wounded
and falling from his horse during the battle.*

34

As the battle raged on, Riedesel's Germans began to regroup and push the American troops backward. Seemingly out of nowhere, Benedict Arnold appeared and rallied the Americans. He rode through their ranks, urging them onward. Riedesel was forced to retreat, and the Americans followed. During this charge, Arnold was badly wounded in one leg. An American soldier was about to bayonet the already wounded German who had fired the shot when Arnold stopped him. "Don't hurt him!" the fallen general cried out. "He only did his duty."

When darkness fell over the scene and the soldiers could no longer see, the battle came to an end. Six hundred British and Germans lay dead, with hundreds more wounded. In contrast, only 130 Americans had been killed, wounded, or captured.

Burgoyne saw that he had only two options—make a run for it or surrender. Either way, he realized to his shame and regret, the British plan to split the colonies in half had failed miserably.

THE BRITISH SURRENDER

During the night of October 7, 1777, the soldiers in General Burgoyne's camp were gripped by feelings of shock and distress. They had been defeated by an army that they considered inferior. British morale sank even lower when,

Soldiers at British camp were in low spirits after the Battle of Saratoga.

the next morning, Burgoyne ordered all able-bodied men to retreat northward. He announced that the dead and wounded would be left behind. That only increased the general mood of despair.

What Burgoyne did not realize was that retreat was now impossible. Gates had stationed militiamen and Continentals on both sides of the river, blocking all escape routes. This left the British in a grave situation. Burgoyne, not knowing that General Clinton had turned back, still believed help was coming. However, even if Clinton really was on the way, his forces were small. Meanwhile, Burgoyne's men were out of supplies.

Burgoyne reluctantly agreed to discuss surrendering to Gates on October 14. The American general made harsh demands, declaring that with "Their provisions exhausted ... their retreat cut off ... they [the British] can only be allowed to surrender as prisoners of war." Gates wanted the British to stack their weapons in a pile in their camp and march out unarmed. But Burgoyne's officers saw

The British soldiers were forced to surrender their weapons after marching from camp.

this as humiliating. Burgoyne later wrote that his troops told him that "they would rather die than accept such dishonorable conditions."

Gates eventually agreed that the defeated soldiers would be allowed to leave camp with their weapons. They would then surrender the weapons to their own officers, who would later turn them over to the Americans. The British officers would permanently retain their swords. On October 17, the British marched out of camp and

The Battle of Saratoga showed the world's great powers that the Americans should not be underestimated.

General Burgoyne surrendered to General Gates on October 17, 1777.

walked between lines of American soldiers, their uniforms

tattered but their heads held high.

Burgoyne approached Gates, who told him, "I am

glad to see you." The British general replied, "I am not glad to see you. It is my fortune, sir, and not my fault that I am here." Burgoyne handed his sword to Gates, signifying the surrender. Gates soon handed it back, honoring the agreement.

Nearly 5,800 British and German troops surrendered that day. The news delighted Americans across the colonies. Meanwhile, European leaders were shocked that the Americans had defeated and captured an entire British army. This victory persuaded France to enter the war on America's side.

French military aid would prove crucial in Britain's ultimate defeat in the Revolutionary War. In that sense, the American victory at Saratoga helped make the survival and freedom of the United States possible.

GLOSSARY

battalion—army unit consisting of a headquarters and three companies of soldiers

battery—groups of heavy guns arranged in one spot

cannon train—group of horse-drawn wagons carrying cannons, accompanied by cannon operators and their supplies

colonies—lands settled by people from another country and ruled by that country

Continental Army—full-time members of the American army during the Revolutionary War

fortifications—buildings or walls built as military defenses

guerrilla tactics—warfare using small, surprise attacks rather than large battles

mercenaries—hired soldiers

morale—the state of a person's or group's spirits

rifling—set of spiral grooves inside the barrel of a firearm

DID YOU KNOW?

- British losses in the battles fought at Lexington and Concord in April 1775 were 73 dead and 174 wounded. The colonists suffered almost 100 men killed, wounded, or missing.

- American General Benedict Arnold was wounded in one leg while fighting the British in 1775. Thereafter he walked with a limp. In the Battle of Saratoga in 1777, he was wounded again in the same leg.

- Captain David Monin, one of the British officers killed by Morgan's riflemen at Freeman's Farm, died fighting beside his 11-year-old son.

- According to an eyewitness account by an American who fought at Saratoga, both American and British soldiers fought bravely. Burgoyne's men were "bold, intrepid, and fought like heroes, [while] our men were equally bold and courageous ... fighting for their all."

- Each year, re-enactment groups, such as the 25th Continental Regiment and 2nd Continental Artillery, stage mock versions of the battles at Freeman's Farm and Bemis Heights. Another re-enactment group, Morgan's Rifles, tours historic battlefields where Morgan and his men fought.

43

IMPORTANT DATES

Timeline

1776
On July 4, the 13 American colonies declare their independence from Britain, marking the official start of the Revolutionary War and the birth of the United States.

1777
In July, Britain's General John Burgoyne leads an army from Canada into upstate New York. On August 19, American General Horatio Gates takes charge of American forces and prepares to fight back. On September 19, Burgoyne's forces attack the Americans at Freeman's Farm, near Saratoga. On October 7, Burgoyne's army assaults Bemis Heights and the British are defeated. Burgoyne surrenders to Gates on October 17.

1783
The United States and Britain sign the Treaty of Paris, which officially ends the Revolutionary War.

1787
The American founding fathers draft the U.S. Constitution.

IMPORTANT PEOPLE

GENERAL HORATIO GATES (1726–1806)

Commander of the American forces at Saratoga; though he was applauded for his victory at Saratoga, his reputation suffered when he was defeated by the British in 1780

GENERAL JOHN BURGOYNE (1722–1792)

Commander of the British forces at Saratoga; after returning home in disgrace following his defeat at Saratoga, he became a playwright

MAJOR GENERAL BENEDICT ARNOLD (1741–1801)

American military officer who turned traitor in 1779 and tried to help the British; today his name is still associated with treason

DANIEL MORGAN (1736–1802)

American soldier who commanded sharpshooting riflemen in battle; he fought in several other battles following Saratoga, and was one of the commanders in the Battle of Cowpens in 1781

MAJOR GENERAL BENJAMIN LINCOLN (1733–1810)

American commander of the New England militia; in 1781, George Washington asked him to accept the British general's surrender sword at Yorktown, the last major battle of the war.

45

WANT TO KNOW MORE?

At the Library

Black, Jeremy. *Warfare in the Eighteenth Century*. New York: Collins/Smithsonian, 2006.

Nardo, Don. *The American Revolution*. San Diego: KidHaven Press, 2002.

Schanzer, Rosalyn. *George vs. George: The Revolutionary War as Seen by Both Sides*.
    Washington, D.C.: National Geographic, 2004.

On the Web

For more information on this topic, use FactHound.

1. Go to *www.facthound.com*

2. Type in this book ID: 0756533422

3. Click on the *Fetch It* button.

FactHound will find the best Web sites for you.

On the Road

Saratoga National Historical Park
648 Route 32
Stillwater, NY 12170
518/664-9821, ext. 224
Battlefields where the British and
American soldiers fought in 1777

New York State Military Heritage Institute
61 Lake Ave.
Saratoga Springs, NY 12866
518/226-0991
Cannons, sabers, and other weapons
used in battles of the Revolutionary
War battles and other U.S. wars

Look for more We the People books about this era:

The Articles of Confederation
The Battle of Bunker Hill
The Battles of Lexington and Concord
The Bill of Rights
The Boston Massacre
The Boston Tea Party
The Declaration of Independence
The Electoral College

Great Women of the American Revolution
The Minutemen
Monticello
Mount Vernon
Paul Revere's Ride
The Surrender of Cornwallis
The U.S. Constitution

A complete list of We the People titles is available on our Web site:
www.compasspointbooks.com

INDEX

About the Author

Historian and award-winning author Don Nardo has written many books for young people about American history. He lives with his wife, Christine, in Massachusetts.